BMX
FREESTYLE

LARRY DANE BRIMNER

BMX FREESTYLE

FRANKLIN WATTS
NEW YORK LONDON SYDNEY TORONTO
1987 A FIRST BOOK

THIS BOOK
PURCHASED BY
MALHEUR COUNTY

Diagrams on pages 49 and 50 are courtesy of
Bob Haro, redrawn by Vantage Art, Inc.

Cover photograph courtesy of © James Cassimus.

Photographs courtesy of: John Ker/BMX Plus!:
pp. 2, 12, 17, 19, 40, 41, 43, 44, 45, 46;
© Jim Cassimus: pp. 28, 29, 35, 36, 39;
Sue Head/"Reynoldsburg Reporter": p. 56;
Mike Toth: p. 59.

Library of Congress Cataloging-in-Publication Data

Brimner, Larry Dane.
BMX freestyle.

(A First book)
Includes index.
Summary: An introduction to performing stunts and routines on motocross bicycles with instructions for tricks and advice on equipment, safety, and competitions.
1. Bicycle motocross—Juvenile literature.
[1. Bicycle motocross] I. Title.
GV1049.3.B73 1987   796.6   86-23355
ISBN 0-531-10301-3

Text copyright © 1987 by Larry Dane Brimner
All rights reserved
Printed in the United States of America
5 4 3 2 1

ACKNOWLEDGMENTS

For their help with research for this book,
grateful thanks to the following:
the American Freestyle Association;
Randy Bowser; Jim Gregg; Judy Griffin;
Phil Gwen; Haro Designs, Inc.; Bill Hawkins;
the National Freestyle Association;
Bob Osborn; Skyway Recreation Products; the
Sprocket Rockets BMX Freestyle Trick Team;
Don Toshach; Trish Walsh; and
Zumwalt's North Park Cycle Co.

Special thanks to Bob Haro and to
Wizard Publications, Inc., for sharing
their stunts with me.

Special thanks also to Randy Loop of
Freestyle Attractions for his valuable
information and encouragement during
the development of this book.

To
Steven Hugh Brimner

CONTENTS

Chapter One
How Freestyle Began
11

Chapter Two
Choosing the Right Bike
15

Chapter Three
Safety Equipment
21

Chapter Four
Avoiding Injuries
23

Chapter Five
How to Begin
26

Chapter Six
Techniques
31

Chapter Seven
Build Your Own Ramp
48

Chapter Eight
Routines
52

Chapter Nine
Teams
54

Chapter Ten
Competition and Organizations
58

Chapter Eleven
Freestyling for Money
61

Chapter Twelve
The Law and Freestyle
64

Chapter Thirteen
Publications
66

Index 69

BMX FREESTYLE

HOW FREESTYLE BEGAN

1

Freestyle bicycle riding had its beginnings in 1976 when teenager Bob Haro grew tired of skateboarding and BMX (Bicycle Motocross) racing. He wanted to do something different, something that would make him stand out from the other kids. His solution: to duplicate skateboard tricks using his bicycle.

Bob's experience in vertical skateboarding made him familiar with skateboard moves, but his first bicycle trick was radical for the time. It took him weeks of practice on a paved hill in front of his house to get the first trick perfected. But after countless failed attempts and a lot of effort, he successfully completed a backward roll.

Today, Haro laughs at the simplicity of his first trick. After all, rolling backward on a bicycle while keeping your balance doesn't involve a lot of complicated maneuvering. And when he compares that first trick with the intricate moves and routines performed by the new generation of riders, he shakes his head in astonishment. Still, that first back-

ward roll opened the way for other tricks, such as roll backs, reverse rock walks, bunny hops, and others.

Bob continued to create and perfect new tricks. He practiced at local skateparks, and he enjoyed the crowds of skateboarders who gathered to watch. Soon some of them traded in their skateboards for BMX bicycles and began practicing with him. The rest is history.

In 1979, Haro took some of his stunts to Bob Osborn, publisher of *BMX Action* magazine, and performed for him. Osborn liked the moves so well that he began running a two-page spread in his magazine featuring the techniques of trick riding. Suddenly, a freestyle professional was born; Bob was earning a living doing what he enjoyed—"showing off" on his bicycle.

That same year, Osborn created the BMX Action Trick Team (now known as the Redline Trick Team). Featuring Bob Haro and Osborn's son, R.L., the team toured the BMX race circuit and performed between heats and at special shows.

Trick riding, or "freestyle," as it came to be called, has grown in popularity ever since. Other kids formed their own teams. They competed against each other to see whose tricks were smoothest, best, and most complex. Today, the number of freestyle riders approaches the number of BMX racers, and there are official competitions scheduled throughout the United States.

Today's routines are more intricate than Haro's early moves. Here Fred Blood zips into one of many track stand variations.

But that isn't all. The rest of the world is out there, too. Bob introduced freestyle to Australia and Canada. And he's made several tours of Europe displaying his stunts and meeting local enthusiasts.

Movies like *E.T.*, which featured Bob and some of his freestyle stunts, and, more recently, *Rad*, have brought freestyle to wide audiences. Is it any wonder that a recent competition at Venice, California, drew entries from all over the world?

CHOOSING THE RIGHT BIKE

2

The right bike is as important to a freestyler as the right racket is to a tennis player. Your choice of a bike depends, in part, on how comfortable you feel on it. If the bike is difficult to maneuver through simple moves, you should try another brand or size.

Of course, how serious you are about freestyling is also of major importance. If the only stunts you ever plan to perform are wheelies and simple curb endos, then any good-quality twenty-inch (50 cm) BMX race bike will do. If, on the other hand, you want to master the more difficult moves and even to create some of your very own, you'll want a bicycle designed specifically for freestyle.

How does a freestyle bike differ from a BMX race bike? To begin with, the frameset (frame and fork) of a race bike is not suitable for the serious freestyler. A freestyle frameset is sturdier and heavier, in order to accommodate the extra slamming (punishment) the bike is likely to receive. Pay special attention, too, to the weld joints. They must be solid and strong to resist cracking.

BRAKES

The most obvious difference between a freestyle bike and a BMX race bike is the braking setup. The serious freestyle bike is equipped with three sets of brakes: front and rear calipers (hand brakes) and a coaster brake. A coaster brake, when it is in its neutral position, allows the bike to travel forward or backward without the pedals rotating.

Three brakes may seem excessive. But to open up the entire world of freestyle, they are necessary. Front endos are impossible without front calipers, while rear calipers are essential to many ramp tricks. The rear coaster brake can be used when it's impractical to use the rear caliper. It takes time, but you'll eventually master their smooth operation.

Many of the new freestyle bikes are also equipped with a device that allows the calipers to be disengaged during a 360-degree (full circle) front wheel spin. Mounted to the handlebar stem, it prevents cable tangle and is a nice accessory, if not a necessity.

WHEELS

With the possible exception of handlebar grips and pedals, wheels take more of a beating than any other part of a bicycle. Toughness and durability should be major considerations.

Basically, you have two selections for freestyle riding: plastic mag wheels or spoked alloys. Spoked alloy wheels are more reasonable in price, but they are also more susceptible

Champion rider Eddie Fiola shows why freestyle bikes have to be solid.

to thrashing (bending and breaking). Plastic mag wheels are made of a blend of Zytel and glass reinforced nylon that makes for a lightweight product that is strong, dependable, and relatively maintenance-free. (Tuff Wheels II is one popular brand.)

Before making a decision, remember that the more involved and advanced in freestyle you become, the more punishment the wheels will take because the stunts you'll perform will push their limits. A good investment at the outset may prove wise in the long run.

TIRES

Freestyle tires are asked to perform a completely different task from BMX racing tires. Stunts performed on hard asphalt and concrete require tires with higher air pressure and less pronounced tread. Bob Haro runs a regular street tire on the rear and a tire with snake belly tread in the front. Other freestylers run stadium-type tires front and rear. Whatever the choice, racing knobbies are *not* for the freestyler. They tend to slide out or hang up during critical moves—something no freestyler wants.

PEDALS

As mentioned, pedals need to be sturdy because they take constant slamming. The selection is almost endless, so look

Special accessories make many acrobatic stunts possible. Note the framestands.

for something basic (steel) and avoid the alloys. They just don't stand the test.

So much for the basic bike. The acrobatics associated with some freestyle moves require special accessories. Forkstands, for instance, make it possible for the rider to straddle the front wheel. Framestands at the rear wheel perform the same function. Axle extenders (pegs) are an alternative to forkstands and framestands. As their name implies, they screw on to the front and rear axles. Many bikes built specifically for freestyle already come with built-in pegs.

The freestyle seatpost is another accessory that may or may not be needed. Freestyle bikes generally have a footstand built in with an extension of the frame below and behind the seat. If your frame lacks this, the freestyle seatpost has a metal loop attached to the post and can be used in the same way. Or a seatpost clamp with a platform can be attached.

These accessories are not required to begin basic freestyle moves. They are needed *only* for some of the more advanced acrobatic stunts.

Using these guidelines, you could build your own bike, but that isn't a requirement. Several companies produce quality bikes geared to freestyling. And so great is the demand, virtually every major manufacturer of bicycles now markets or plans to market a line for freestyle. Prices range from $150 to $700, but you need not enter bankruptcy for a decent bike. A bike suitable for competition should run around $200 to $250.

Whether you build one or purchase a prebuilt machine, one rule should be remembered: Strength and quality determine longevity.

SAFETY EQUIPMENT

3

Like any sport, freestyle carries with it a certain amount of risk. Bob Osborn reminds people of an old adage about BMX racing: "Whatever you don't protect is where you're gonna land." It's as true for freestyle as it is for BMX racing.

THE RIDER

Freestylers accept the fact that they'll be falling often while they learn the sport. The best way to avoid injury is to dress accordingly. Your body—and your mother—will thank you.

Recommended gear includes a protective helmet, a mouth guard, padded gloves, long pants, a jersey or long-sleeve shirt, tennis shoes, ankle guards, and elbow and forearm guards. These are available from a variety of manufacturers in several styles and at a range of prices.

If you want to look like the freestylers you see on television, in magazines, or at exhibitions, you'll want specially designed pants and jersey with built-in padding to protect the shins, knees, rump, forearms, and elbows. They're expensive, but you'll look like a pro.

THE MACHINE

No matter how much protection you wear on your body, you'll want some on your bike as well. No, it's not to protect the bike. It's to protect *you.*

Apply knee bumpers (safety pads) to the handlebars, crossbar, stem, and frame. They wrap around those parts of the bike that you're likely to encounter in a mishap and fasten with either snaps or Velcro. Available in an assortment of colors, they give your bike that customized look. Mark this item as essential. You'll fall on a bare frame only once.

AVOIDING INJURIES

4

Accidents occur in all sports, and freestyling is no exception. However, your chances of experiencing a serious injury will be greatly reduced if you (1) think ahead and (2) practice safety. As with any strenuous activity, stretching and warm-up will help your body adjust to the demands you'll be making on it. Learn stunts at your own pace; don't be pressured into doing something you're not ready for. Make sure your practice area is free of obstacles and hazards, and protect yourself by wearing appropriate clothing at all times.

Kick turns and aerials off a quarter-pipe are dramatic, and you're going to want to learn them first. Don't. You'll save yourself time and possible injury if you stick with something basic at first. Decide on a trick that you feel you're capable of performing, and practice until you get it right. Don't jump from trick to trick. Master one before proceeding to the next.

Learn the basics first. Randy Loop, director of the Sprocket Rockets BMX Freestyle Trick Team, suggests beginning with the KISS method: *Keep It Simple Stupid*. Try a simple trick. If it fails, analyze it. Then try it again without repeating the mistake.

It will probably be easiest if you begin with the ground tricks. Once you have mastered these, you can move on to easy tricks on the small ramp. When you feel comfortable on the small ramp, move on to the quarter-pipe. But don't be in a rush. Rome wasn't conquered in a day, and neither will freestyle be mastered in a day.

Practice in a safe area. To begin with, practice on bike paths, paved playgrounds, or outdoor basketball courts. Once you're ready for advanced stunts, you can take advantage of skateparks that allow freestylers or even an empty swimming pool. Always practice on a hard surface like a cement driveway or a paved, unused parking lot. Be sure the area is clear of any broken glass, large rocks, or sharp objects that might be a hazard. Although freestyle began in the street, never practice in an area with traffic. It's rumored that speeding cars can be hazardous to your health! And *never* practice in a blind roadway where you can't see oncoming traffic.

When you're ready to practice with a ramp, be sure it butts against something solid so it won't move or tilt. Ramp riding is the most dangerous type of freestyling, so give yourself time to feel comfortable with it. Be patient.

It may seem cool to pop a boomerang as you leave school, and it might impress your friends, but unless you're dressed for the activity, don't do it. Accidents happen when you least expect them. Although protective clothing (Chapter 3) won't make you invincible to injury, it will give you some extra padding to absorb the blow of a fall. And if you're plagued by "pizza knees," it means you haven't padded the handlebars, crossbar, stem, and frame of your machine. It should wear protective "clothing," too.

Some riders use the buddy system when practicing. They have a couple of friends hold the bike up so they can get the "feel" of a trick before they actually try it. This might prove helpful in mastering some of the tricks and is worth consideration.

Failure is part of learning. While you're learning freestyle, you'll probably fail more often than not—at least in the beginning—so get comfortable with the idea. Learn to fall. Instinct will tell you when you're out of control and it's time to abort. When that time comes, it's best to spring from the bike and try to land on your feet. Only hold on to your bike if it helps you regain body control. If it's not going to help, let the bike go, and don't worry about it. It's built for slamming; you're not. A rule: Worry about yourself first, your bike later.

Be rested when you practice. If you get tired while you're practicing, take a break. Freestyle is a strenuous sport, and there's no sense in complicating matters by practicing when you're tired.

Remember that freestyle is gymnastics and acrobatics on a bike. Take it slow at first. Be aware of your own limitations and abilities. "Perform" each trick mentally before you try it physically. Try to anticipate and avoid difficulties, and before long you'll be able to string your tricks together into a routine.

HOW TO BEGIN

5

Time and practice are the key elements to successful freestyling. In the beginning, Bob Haro developed freestyle by making up tricks and practicing until he could do them. Today, thirteen-year-old Scott Freeman rides for the Skyway Trick Team because he practices five to six hours per day. The freestylers you see in movies, commercials, and magazines got there because they practiced until they were good—and then they practiced some more. With some dedicated time, you'll be *scootin'* around with slick moves, too.

Not everyone has equal ability. What is easy for one person will be difficult for another. You should begin at the beginning; however, where *you* begin may be different from where someone else begins. That's okay as long as the trick you choose to begin with is basic for you. Stick with it until you get it right, then go on to learn another move. The tricks described in this book are arranged according to level of difficulty—from easy to difficult—but that arrangement is only a guideline.

Before attempting any trick, be sure you are dressed appropriately (Chapter 3). Apply safety padding to your bike, and remove hazards from your practice area. Then mentally think through each trick before you actually practice it.

Don't worry if your trick isn't exactly like somebody else's. Each person rides differently, and each person puts individual style into a trick. Freestyling is anything and everything you want it to be. It is a form of self-expression. When you become really comfortable performing a trick, you'll begin to inject it with a little of your own style. Then you'll be *shreddin' heavily*—a compliment to any freestyler.

Most riders already perform some freestyle, whether they know it or not. The two most basic moves of freestyle are the wheelie and the curb endo. Learning these two tricks is a good place to begin.

WHEELIE • Begin the wheelie by riding seated. Pull back on the handlebars to lift the front wheel off the ground while you continue to pedal. As the bike reaches the balance point, push or pull with your arms to keep it there. Continue to ride the rear wheel. If you sense the bike is going all the way over, step off and try it again.

You can add some style to this trick by riding one-hand or one-foot.

The coaster wheelie is the same trick, only it's done while coasting downhill.

CURB ENDO • You might want to try the buddy system (Chapter 4) with the curb endo to get the feel of this trick before you attempt it on your own. Begin by approaching the curb slowly. Aim the bike as straight at the curb as pos-

Above: the wheelie. Opposite: the more stretched out you are, the higher your curb endo will be!

sible. Your body should be in a seated position, and the pedals should be in neutral (level or horizontal). As the front tire gently touches the curb, spring upward (stand) and push the handlebars forward with your arms. The rear of the bike will lift off the ground.

Let the bike come up by bending your knees. With arms extended, stretch back over the rear wheel. The more stretched out you are, the higher the rear wheel will lift. If you sense you're going all the way over, step over the handlebars.

Keep your arms stiff to keep the bike from swinging left or right. The point of this trick is to hang in the air as long as possible before gravity takes its course.

When the rear of the bike begins to drop, imagine that you are setting it down on eggs. As the wheel touches down, shift your body back to the seat. Making sure the pedals are level, pull back on the handlebars to begin a backward roll. Then pop the front wheel off the ground, turn the handlebar left or right, do a turn on the rear wheel, and pedal out of your curb endo.

When you get comfortable with the basic curb endo, you might want to try variations. They include no-curb (using the front caliper to stop), one-hand, no-hand, no-feet. But these are very dangerous and complicated feats and require a great deal of experience and skill.

TECHNIQUES

6

In freestyle you have to keep practicing until your bike and body move as one unit. It's easy to become discouraged. The ten tricks outlined in this chapter have been laid out in as simple and safe a manner as possible. You may know of a safer or better way to perform them. Or you may find some of the intermediate tricks easier to learn than the beginner tricks. If this is the case, don't be afraid to do it your way. That's what freestyle is about!

BEGINNER

TRACK STAND • Track stands are balancing tricks or poses, and no special equipment is needed. However, you must be able to grasp both the grip of the handlebar and the seat with one hand when the front wheel is turned at 90 degrees.

Start out by slowly riding forward with both hands on the handlebars and standing on the pedals. The left pedal should be all the way down. Lift your right leg over the top tube, and rest your right foot at the bottom of the front triangle formed by the frame (where the pedal cranks join the frame).

Using your front brake, come to a full stop and turn your front wheel 90 degrees. With your right hand, grip the end of the handlebar and the seat. At the same time, move your left foot to the front tire and release the brake as soon as your foot is in place. The bike will be tilted at about 45 degrees and your body will form a rough *U*. Balance by using your left foot to roll the front tire forward or backward.

For the trickiest maneuver, quickly move your left hand from the grip to the front tire while putting your left foot back on the left pedal. Let the bike drop slightly. Use your left hand to roll the bike back and forth to maintain your balance.

Putting all your weight on your left foot, bring your right foot up and over the top tube but under the right grip and seat. Tighten your right leg so that it's stiff, and use your right foot to lock the handlebars in place.

Take your hands from their respective positions and lean back slightly. As you lean back, the bike will lift. Be careful not to go completely backward. For the finale, spread your arms out and balance.

BUNNY HOP • Bunny hops are jumping tricks. Begin by hopping over nothing at all. Then try jumping small objects like curbs or shoeboxes. Cardboard boxes are especially nice because they collapse if you goof.

Think small in the beginning. Then when your abilities and coordination have improved, go to something a little taller. Keep building. Before long, you'll be hopping benches or even taller obstacles. Just don't get ahead of yourself because failure at this trick can mean disaster for your body.

Approach the obstacle you wish to hop at moderate speed with the pedals level. Start coasting several feet before the obstacle, and time your jump.

Pull up on the handlebars while moving your body up and forward. As the front of the bike lifts, prepare to raise the rear by dipping your rump over the back wheel. Pull up with your arms, and let the bike come into your body by flexing your knees.

When you've cleared the obstacle, lift your body and straighten your legs to push the rear of the bike down so you'll land on the rear wheel. Continue pulling on the handlebars to keep up the front end. As you touch down, flex your knees to absorb the shock.

POGO • Another jumping trick, though of a different kind, is the pogo. It is widely used in flatland competition, and variations are numerous. At competitions you'll see riders pogoing on the rear wheel, the front wheel, and both wheels. You'll also see departures from this as they use their imagination to pogo with their own style.

For the basic rear wheel pogo, begin by standing with one foot on the back pedal to activate the rear coaster brake. Place your other foot on the other pedal. Lean backward and pull back on the handlebars (as if you were doing a wheelie). The coaster brake should remain engaged.

Spring up with your body and pull the bike with you. Keep the front end high, and both wheels should become airborne. The harder you pull and lift, the higher you'll pogo. Repeat this process to continue pogoing.

An easier form of this stunt requires the rider to stand with both feet on the rear rim. Hold the bike in a vertical position and bounce up and down, lifting the bike with you—a variation on a theme.

WHEEL STAND • The wheel stand is a trick that will be useful later, when you work with a partner or team. Begin by facing your bike and turning the front wheel 90 degrees to the center. Put your left foot on the front tire as close to the top center as possible.

Squeeze the front caliper to steady the bike. At the same time, grip the end of the handlebars and seat with one hand to provide more stability. Quickly lift your other foot on top of the tire. Release the brake and balance by rolling the tire from side to side. The closer your feet are, the more balance you'll have.

Once you are balanced, remove one hand. Then remove the other hand and stand upright. Use your arms like a tightrope walker and continue to roll the tire from side to side to maintain your balance.

How does a partner figure into this trick? A partner can bunny hop your bike's seat while you balance. But don't try it until your partner can bunny hop at least three feet!

ROCK WALK • Rock walks help you develop balance, control, and self-confidence. And they're one of the easiest tricks to learn.

Begin seated, coasting at a moderate speed. Have the pedals level. Bend your knees a little and lean forward to

The front wheel stand. Note how Bob Haro grips the handlebars and seat with one hand.

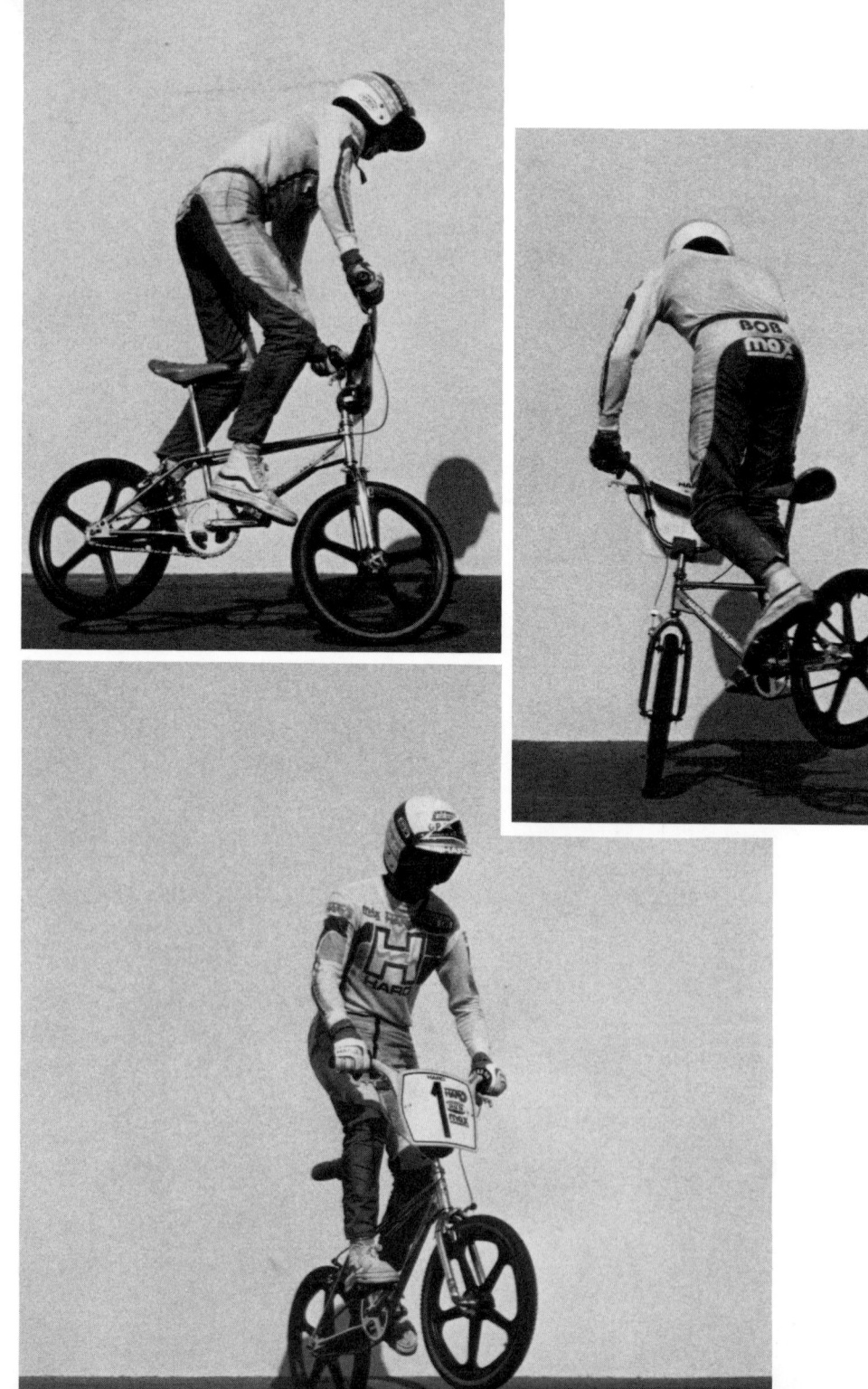

take the weight off the rear end. Turn slightly into the direction of your pivot.

When you begin turning into your pivot, shift your weight to the handlebars by straightening your legs and leaning forward. As you do this, move your hips to the side, and catch the seat with your knee. Use your knee to flip the rear of the bike into a 180-degree rotation (half circle) around the front end. Pedals should be kept level.

As the rear touches down, shift your weight back to the center of the bike and pull back on the handlebars. Begin pedaling forward. This will cause the front end to come up wheelie-style through the final 180 degrees. Keep the front end up as you ride out.

When you have this trick smoothed out, you can string three or four of them together without breaks for a show-stopping stunt. And when you can pull off a multiple rock walk, you're no longer a beginner!

INTERMEDIATE

The tricks in the beginner section are called ground or flatland tricks. They can be performed on any flat, solid surface. The intermediate tricks call for a small ramp. The added height adds to the show, but it also adds risk. Don't attempt the tricks in this section until you feel you're ready. Think through each trick before attempting it so that a clear picture of what you want to happen is in your mind. And as always, dress in complete safety gear.

The rock walk swings through a full circle.

KICK TURN • The kick turn is a basic ramp trick, and it has endless variations. To begin, come up to the ramp at a fairly slow speed, standing. (Until you get used to ramp riding, remain in the lower regions of the ramp.) Have your pedals level.

As you approach the spot where you want to start your turn, slightly steer your bike into the direction you want to rotate. While you're doing this, you have to ease on the rear brake until the wheel locks, and pull up on the front end, as though attempting a wheelie. Lean to the side and swing the bike around 180 degrees. The higher you lift the front end at the outset, the tighter and faster you'll turn.

As you about-face, lean forward. Release the brake so that the front wheel lightly touches down.

RAMP ENDO • The ramp endo is nothing more than a curb endo on a tilted surface. But since a ramp doesn't have a curb, you'll apply the front caliper to create your stop.

As with all ramp tricks, stay low on the ramp until you gain confidence. Begin by picking out the spot on the ramp where you're going to lock the front brake. Approach that point at a slow speed with the pedals level. It is absolutely critical that the front wheel be straight.

When you reach the spot where you plan to brake, apply and hold the front caliper. At the same time, move your body forward to take the weight off the rear of the bike. Push the handlebars away from you. This will help the rear of the bike to lift.

This rider adds some pizazz to the kick turn finale by "crossing up" the handlebars.

Martin Aparijo uses his arms to get lift in the ramp endo.

    As the rear of the bike comes up, shift your rump back over the rear wheel. Flex your legs to allow the bike to reach the balance point. Hold the balance as long as possible.
    As gravity takes its course, the rear of the bike will begin to drop. Just as it touches down, release the front brake and roll backward down the ramp. For a great finish, turn 180 degrees on the rear wheel (a kick turn on the ground), and continue your ride.

FLASHER
(QUARTER-PIPE)

The ultimate freestyle tricks are flashed on the big ramp or "quarter-pipe." These are the tricks you'll see performed by Eddie Fiola, R. L. Osborn, Hugo Gonzales, and other celebrity riders. To attempt them requires skill, dexterity, and guts!

POP OUT • Approach the ramp at a fairly good speed. Practice will tell you exactly how fast. Stand with pedals level, and lean forward as the bike climbs the ramp. Use your arms to pull the bike up.

As the bike reaches the top of the ramp, twist your bike and body so that you can land on the top of the ramp. Remove your right foot from the pedal, using it to pivot on the platform. As your bike touches down, turn it around to face in the direction from which you just came.

Keep your foot on the rear coaster brake and keep the front wheel high. Extend your arms and shift your weight over the rear tire (keeping the front end high).

Release the rear brake and ride down the ramp.

DROP IN • A drop in is used to enter a bowl at a skatepark or an empty pool. Begin by positioning the rear tire on the edge of the top of the ramp (or bowl). Keep the front end high. Rest one foot on the ramp's platform and the other on the pedal with the coaster brake applied.

Fearless Hugo Gonzales demonstrates a skatepark pop out.

As the bike begins to fall, bring the foot that is on the ground up to the pedal. Keep the coaster brake on, and shift your rump back behind the seat. Use your arms to lower the front end with control.

Release the coaster brake. Extend your arms as the bike touches down, and go into another trick.

AERIAL • An aerial is a 180-degree turn in midair. Begin practicing on the lower portion of the ramp. As you gain confidence and skill, you can increase your altitude.

Ride standing with the pedals level. Get up enough speed so that you can make it halfway up the ramp (more speed when you're ready for higher elevations). If you're going to aerial to the right, ride up the ramp about a foot left of center. If you're going to aerial to the left, reverse that.

As you ride straight up the ramp, you'll begin to slow. At this point, steer slightly into the direction of your turn, and pull the bike into your body by bending your arms and legs. Make your 180-degree turn.

As the bike comes around, straighten your arms and legs to push the bike back down to the ramp. Have both wheels touch down at the same time, then repeat until perfect.

A show-stopping aerial like this one by Tony Murray requires lots of practice and skill.

BUILD YOUR OWN RAMP

7

A full-fledged freestyler eventually will want to ride ramps, but most are not lucky enough to live near skateparks that allow freestylers. Many riders rely on packed dirt, plywood-covered sand, and driveway slopes for small ramp substitutes. For more advanced riders, empty swimming pools make excellent large ramps. In the absence of these devices, however, you can have a quality ramp by building your own. That's right! Some wood, nails, and sweat is all it takes.

SMALL AND LARGE RAMPS

Equipment: power or hand saw, hammer, screwdriver, tape measure, and drill.

Materials: 2" x 4" lumber, 5/8" and 1/2" plywood, wood glue, wood screws, and no. 8 nails.

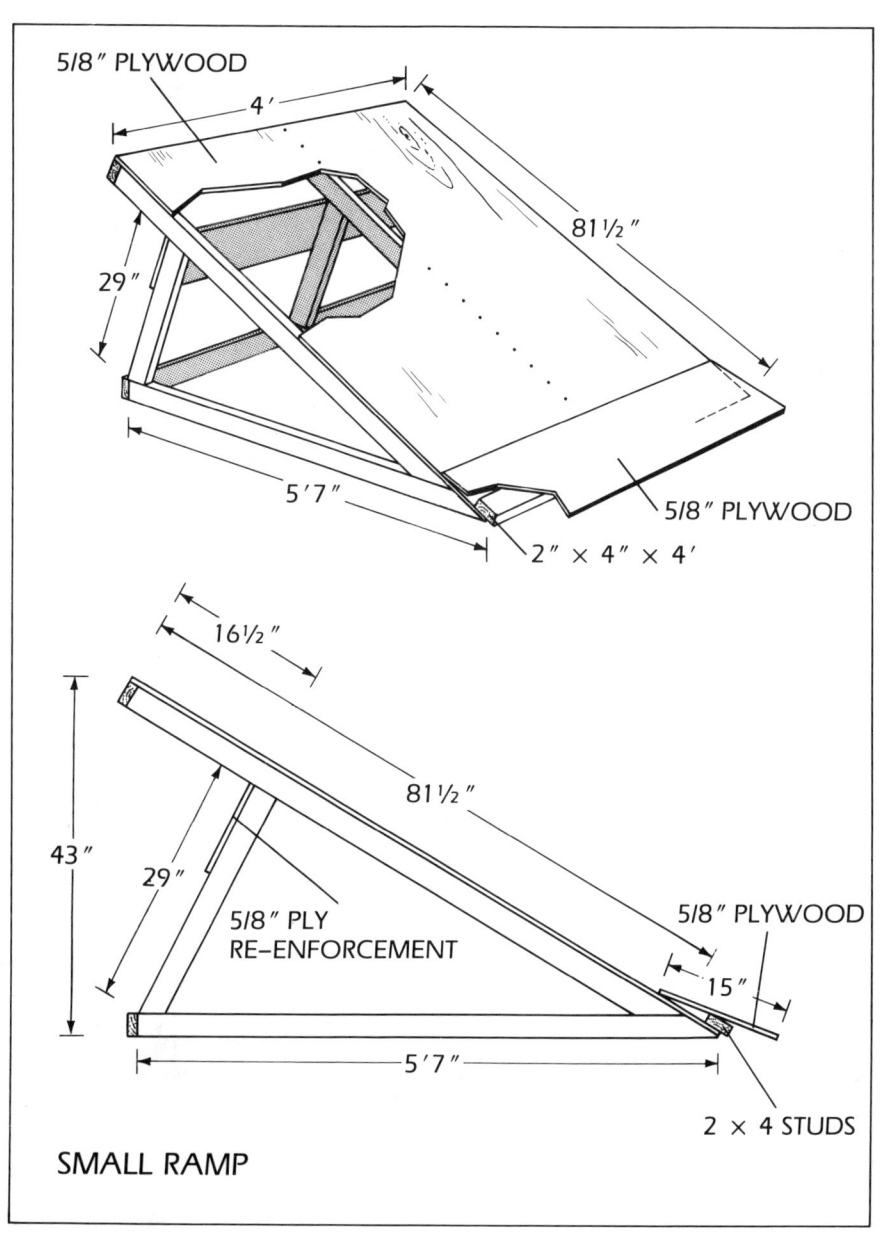

SMALL RAMP

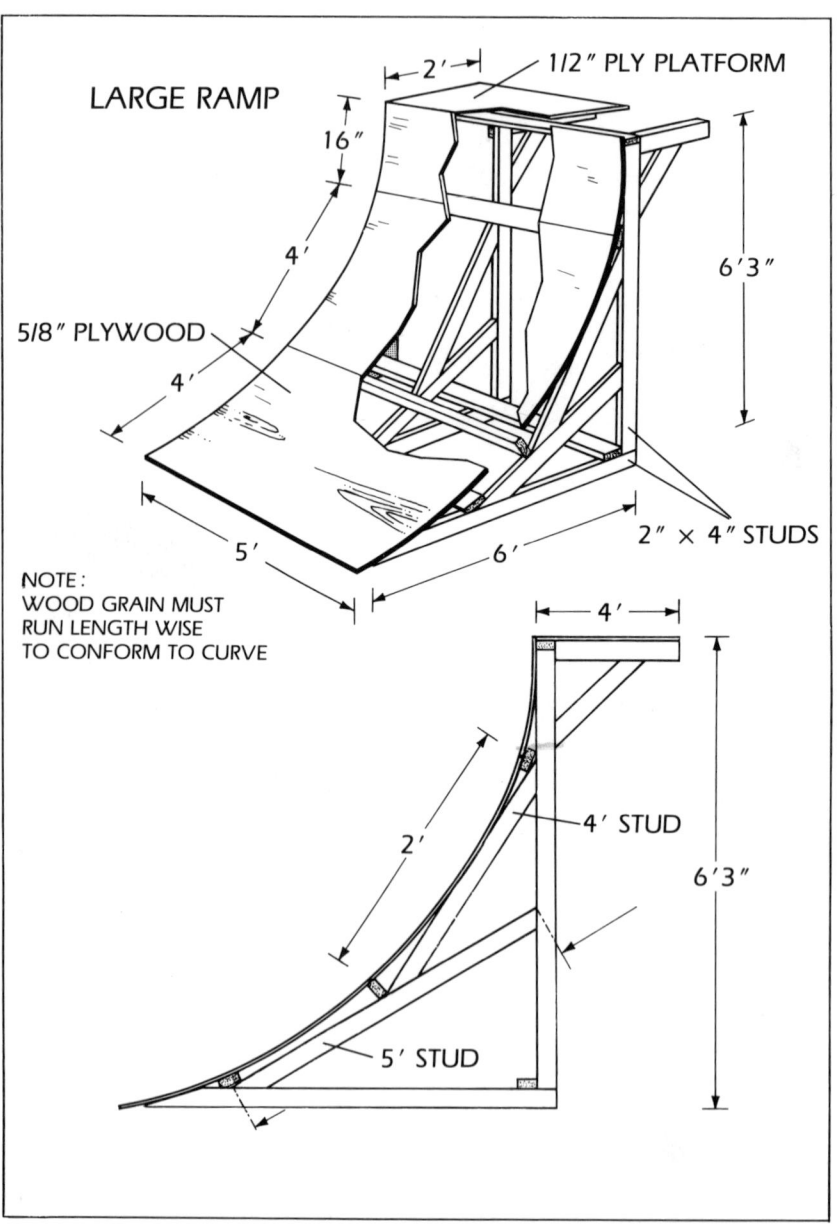

HINTS

All tools should be used with caution. If you're not a carpenter, ask an adult to help you.

You may decide to personalize your ramp with paint. If so, do *not* use glossy paint, as it will cause the tires to slip. It is best to surface the ramp with strips of traction tape or to scratch the riding area with a hammer claw to provide more hold.

Before using a ramp, it should be blocked against something solid. A ramp that is not firmly blocked will tip.

DIRECTIONS

Following the diagrams, cut 2" x 4" lumber to the dimensions specified. Nail the boards together to form the frame. Attach the plywood to the frame with both wood glue and screws for sturdiness.

ROUTINES

8

When you have practiced and are able to perform several tricks smoothly, you'll want to combine them into a routine.

You might practice going from a flatland trick to a ramp trick. Or string together several flatland tricks, and use the ramp for a finale. Or do a kick turn off the small ramp, circle around and pop out off the big ramp, and then pogo or rock walk into a track stand for a finish. The variations are endless. There is no right or wrong way to create routines. Use your imagination.

Use your imagination, too, to create new moves. Only twelve tricks are described in this book. There are literally hundreds, and the number increases every time there is an official competition because freestylers like to show off with something original.

Whether using original tricks, the ones described in this book, or those you've seen other freestylers perform, add class to your act by setting it to music. A nice, bouncy tune is great for the pogo, while something with a dramatic crescendo can highlight a drop in. Any kind of music will do as long as you can get in sync with it. And remember, the music is part of the act, not separate from it. Choose it with as much care as a gymnast or an acrobat—for that is what the freestyler is.

TEAMS

9

Freestyle can be done alone. If you like to cycle and if you also like executing difficult moves, freestyle is for you. For anyone who likes the rhythm of gymnastics and the action of acrobatics, freestyle is a natural. You can work on several of your flashiest tricks and show off your strengths.

But if you like to ride with friends, freestyle can also be done with a partner or team. You and a friend might like to work up a routine where you synchronize your movements. One bike and rider doing a rock walk is quite a sight. When it's done with two bikes and riders in perfect time, the excitement doubles.

Partners can also play against each other to create excitement. One rider can wheel stand while the other bunny hops. Sometimes one rider will turn 180 degrees in one direction while the other will turn in the opposite direction. Partners can open up new dimensions of riding with these imaginative combinations.

Teams usually show off against other teams to see who is better. Sometimes one team member at a time performs his best tricks. At other times, it's like a three-ring circus, giving the audience nonstop entertainment.

Whether you ride with a partner or a complete team, you'll probably want uniforms. You can invest in padded BMX racing pants and jerseys of a certain color. But you needn't spend that kind of money right away. Maybe you'll want to agree on a particular style and color of long-sleeve shirts and pants, then wear your safety gear over these. Whichever route you choose, you'll want to decide on a catchy name or logo that will stand out and be remembered.

Many teams ride with sponsorship. Sponsors agree to help teams meet expenses in exchange for advertising. Sometimes a bicycle shop will agree to sponsor a team, knowing that any shows the shop puts on will draw crowds and possible sales. But sponsors aren't a necessity; any group of friends can ride as a team.

Some teams achieve professional status. The members of professional teams have worked hard to become the best in freestyle, and others have recognized that. Typically, they ride with several sponsors and perform often. The Sprocket Rockets BMX Freestyle Trick Team, for example, performs at over twenty-five shows each year and has been on national television and many newscasts. The Redline Trick Team, sponsored by *BMX Action* and *Freestylin'* magazines, logs 40,000 (64,000 km) miles annually in the United States and travels to Europe five times each year. Similarly, the GT World Tour Team recently went around the world. Other professional trick teams you're likely to hear about are Haro, Skyway, Hutch, and Ground Control.

The Sprocket Rockets, Tony Riddle and Mark Ellis, team up to earn pocket money.

Whether amateur or professional, all teams need leadership. If you create a team or if you join one already formed, make sure that all members' ideas are welcome. Without give and take, teams don't last long.

COMPETITION AND ORGANIZATIONS

10

Competing against other freestylers is a real challenge. You can learn about contests by listening to the radio, reading BMX and freestyle magazines, and inquiring at your local bike shop.

In contests, riders bring out their best tricks to impress the judges. First prize may be a lot of money. The 1985 AFA Freestyle Masters Championship had a $5,000 purse. Prize amounts keep growing, but usually riders compete for trophies, ribbons, or freestyle equipment.

Sometimes riders are more interested in the audience at a contest than in the prizes. Since freestylers are considered old-timers at the age of twenty-five, the professional teams are always looking for new blood. Scouts frequent the big freestyle events searching for new talent, and they may offer a contract when they see someone who has potential.

When competing, you don't have to perform only risky and difficult tricks. Judges look for smoothness and creativity as well. It's better to perform a simple trick rhythmically than to perform a difficult one awkwardly.

The cherry picker. Tony Riddle shows how to impress judges with this smooth track stand.

Freestylers can compete alone or as members of a team. They can compete in flatland events or ramp events or both. Usually, however, riders specialize. It's difficult to be a master of all. Contestants compete against others of the same age. Classes are divided between amateurs and professionals.

Two organizations sanction freestyle contests: the American Freestyle Association (AFA) and the National Freestyle Association (NFA). The AFA operates the "Freestyle Masters Series" and "King of the Skateparks" events. Although it holds competitions for amateurs, it more widely attracts riders who have already achieved professional standing.

The NFA sanctions more grassroots competition for amateurs than the AFA. Its intention is to work with beginning freestylers and to bring them up to professional status. The NFA schedules events often and in numerous locations so that freestyle competitions will be convenient to as many riders as possible.

Although both organizations sanction competitions in the United States, they also have affiliates in several other countries as well. The addresses of the AFA and NFA are given below. Write to them for schedules and membership information.

American Freestyle Association
P.O. Box 2339
Cypress, California 90630

National Freestyle Association
4030 Benson Avenue
Baltimore, Maryland 21227

FREESTYLING FOR MONEY

11

Not everyone can earn money while doing something that brings self-fulfillment. Bob Haro is an exception; he turned his love of freestyle into a multimillion-dollar business. He's not alone. Others have turned their freestyling ability into a money-making venture. And you can, too.

The most obvious way a freestyler can make money is to become a member of a professional team. Some teams pay their thirteen-, fourteen-, and fifteen-year-old riders $15,000, $30,000, and even $40,000 per year. If that's your goal, go for it. Practice, practice, practice until every move is perfect, and then try to get picked up by a team.

Getting a team to recognize you isn't as difficult as you might think. Scouts haunt contests and send names of potential riders to team captains. But some freestylers take the offensive. They approach teams themselves and ask to show off their tricks. This tactic often works, for many teams are eager to see new talent. Other riders hire photographers to take pictures of their action tricks. Then they send the photos to the team with a short autobiography and request for a "tryout." The addresses of most teams are listed in BMX and freestyle magazines.

Freestyle stars also make money by endorsements. They allow their pictures and names to be used in advertisements for products. Some have turned to the big money of television commercials. But these riders didn't start out filming commercials and posing for advertisements. They started out like everyone else—learning the basic wheelie and curb endo—and kept adding to their routines until they were ultrasmooth.

Though they usually pay off in trophies and ribbons, many contests offer prize money. If you are a professional, a contest can be a way of picking up some quick cash over a weekend. Even if you don't win, contests offer valuable experience.

There are other ways to earn money freestyling without breaking into the big time. Most communities of any size have bicycle shops, and some would be willing to pay a talented freestyler for a performance that would draw customers into the shop. Of course, it would be helpful if the bicycle dealer sells freestyle bikes.

One advantage that BMX freestyle has over BMX racing is that freestyle doesn't require a track. Flatland tricks can be performed almost anywhere there is a flat surface. Ramps can be toted by anyone who has access to a truck. Use this to your advantage; become an entrepreneur. Get together with some of your friends and hire them for your own trick team. Then go around to bicycle shops and shopping malls in your area and stimulate some interest. Suggest a performance. What about during intermission or half-time at local sporting events? Of course, if you form your own team, be fair with the division of money, or you might end up with no team at all.

With your freestyle skill and some imagination, there is plenty of opportunity to turn your hobby into a money-making business venture.

THE LAW AND FREESTYLE

12

Freestyle is a great way for you to display cycling talent and coordination, but sometimes it can make you enemies if you don't obey the law. Become familiar with the bicycle rules in your community so that you don't accidentally become a victim of ignorance.

Most laws are based on common sense. If you think before acting, most embarrassing situations can be avoided. Sidewalks, for example, may seem like the ideal places to freestyle. But if you zip by a senior citizen or startle a small child, their surprise reaction may throw you off balance and create a hazardous situation for all. It's better to stay clear of sidewalks and leave them to pedestrians.

As cycling has grown in popularity, many communities have set aside bike paths or bikeways. Generally, bicyclists adhere to the same rules as automobile drivers. If you think of a bike path as a mini-roadway, you'll be thinking smart. At no time should you block a bike path to perform your freestyle tricks. Instead, look for one that isn't heavily traveled so that you can freestyle without being an obstacle. If you aren't always on the lookout for traffic, you'll be able to concentrate more on your moves.

Freestyle had its origin in the road. But that doesn't mean you should perform stunts down the center of Main Street. If you do, your parents might get a call requesting them to pick you up at the local police station. Street riding should be done only on roads with no traffic and an unobstructed field of vision. If a car does come along, move out of the way. If you or the crowd watching you blocks traffic, you may be heading for a close encounter of the legal kind.

Public parks sometimes have areas that are suitable for freestyling. However, some parks have laws prohibiting bikes, roller skates, and skateboards. If your neighborhood park has such a rule, you can try to get it changed. But in the meantime, obey the law.

Private property is a good place to practice freestyle. Large paved or cement driveways are perfect. Unused parking lots are good, too. Just remember, though, that if the property doesn't belong to you, you should get permission before using it. And if at any time you are told to move on, do so.

If you show people that you are a responsible rider by demonstrating courtesy and safety, they usually will not object to your freestyle practice. And they may even become freestyle enthusiasts.

PUBLICATIONS

By ou may want to pursue your interest in freestyle. The following list of books and magazines may help.

BOOKS

Haro, Bob. *Freestyle Moves.* Haro Designs, Inc., 1982.

Osborn, Bob. *The Complete Book of BMX.* Harper and Row, 1984.

MAGAZINES

BMX Action
3162 Kashiwa Street
Torrance, California 90505

BMX Action Bike
134 Tooley Street
London, England SE 1

BMX Bi-Weekly
Market Street
Morecambe, Lancashire, England LA4 5DN

BMX Plus!
P.O. Box 9502
Mission Hills, California 91345

Freestyle BMX
Market Street
Morecambe, Lancashire, England LA4 5DN

Freestylin' Magazine
3162 Kashiwa Street
Torrance, California 90505

Super BMX & Freestyle
7950 Deering Avenue
Canoga Park, California 91304

NEWSLETTERS

AFA Aerial Newsletter
P.O. Box 2339
Cypress, California 90630

Northeast Freestyle
32 Mason Road
Whitinsville, Massachusetts 01588

Shreddin' Midwest Newsletter
9 Holly Court
Reynoldsburg, Ohio 43068

INDEX

Illustrations are indicated by italicized page numbers.

Accident prevention. *See* Safety measures
Advertisements, freestyle stars used in, 62
Aerials, 23, *46,* 47
AFA. *See* American Freestyle Association
AFA Freestyle Masters Championship, 58
American Freestyle Association (AFA), 60
Ankle guards, 21
Aparijo, Martin, *40-41*
Axle extenders, 20

Backward roll, 11

Balancing tricks, 31-32
Bicycles. *See* Freestyle bicycles
Bike paths, 64
Blood, Fred, *12*
BMX Action magazine, 13, 55
BMX Action Trick Team, 13
BMX (Bicycle Motocross) racing, 11, 13
   bicycles, 15
   risks, 21
Books, 66
Brakes, 16
Buddy system, 25
Bunny hop, 32-33

Cherry picker, *59*
Clothing, 21-22, 24
   uniforms, 55

Coaster brake, 16
Coaster wheelie, 27
Competition, 14, 58, 60
Curb endos, 15, 27, *29*, 30

Drop in, 42, 47
    music as setting for, 53

Elbow guards, 21
Ellis, Mark, *56*
Endorsements by freestyle stars, 62
Entrepreneurial opportunities, 62-63
E.T. (movie), 14

Falls, 21, 25
Fiola, Eddie, *17*, 42
Flasher tricks. *See* Quarter-pipe tricks
Flatland tricks (ground tricks), 24, 31-37, 62
    routines, 52
Footstands, 20
Forearm guards, 21
Forkstands, 20
Frameset, 15
Framestands, *19*, 20
Freeman, Scott, 26
Freestyle bicycle riding
    beginner tricks, 31-37
    competition, 14, 58, 60
    earning money from, 61-63
    how to begin, 26-30
    intermediate tricks, 37-41
    legal aspects, 64-65
    organizations, 60
    origin of, 11-14
    publications, 66-67
    routines, 52-53
    safety equipment, 21-22
    safety measures, 23-25
    teams, 54-57
    techniques, 31-47
Freestyle bicycles, 15
    brakes, 16
    choosing a bicycle, 15-20
    frameset, 15
    pedals, 18, 20
    prices, 20
    safety pads, 22
    special accessories, 20
    tires, 18
    wheels, 16, 18
Freestylin' magazine, 55
Freestyle Masters Series, 60
Front calipers, 16
Front endos, 16
Front wheel spin, 16, *35*

Gloves, 21

Gonzales, Hugo, 42, *43-45*
Ground tricks. *See* Flatland tricks
GT World Tour Team, 55

Hand brakes, 16
Haro, Bob, 11, 13-14, 18, 26, 61
   wheel stand, *35*
Helmets, 21

Intermediate tricks, 37-41
Injuries, prevention of. *See* Safety measures

Jumping tricks, 32-34

Kick turns, 23, 38, *39*
King of the Skateparks, 60
KISS method of learning tricks, 24
Knee bumpers, 22

Legal aspects of freestyling, 64-65
Loop, Randy, 23

Magazines, 66-67
Money-making business, freestyling as a, 61-63
Mouth guards, 21
Murray, Tony, *46*

Music, freestyle tricks set to, 52-53

National Freestyle Association (NFA), 60
Newsletters, 67
NFA. *See* National Freestyle Association
No-curb trick, 30

Organizations, 60
Osborn, Bob, 13, 21
Osborn, R.L., 13, 42

Pedals, 18, 20
Pegs (axle extenders), 20
"Pizza knees," 24
Plastic mag wheels, 16, 18
Pogo, 33-34, 53
Pop out, 42, *43-45*
Prizes, 58, 62
Professional teams, 55, 61
Protective clothing, 21-22, 24, 55
Publications, 66-67
Public parks, 65

Quarter-pipe tricks, 23-24, 42-47

Rad (movie), 14
Ramp endo, 38, *40-41*, 41
Ramps, building of, 48-51

Ramp tricks, 24, 37-47, 62
    brakes for, 16
    routines, 52
Rear calipers, 16
Redline Trick Team, 13, 55
Riddle, Tony, *56, 59*
Rock walk, 34, *36*, 37
Routines, 52-53

Safety measures
    avoiding injuries, 23-25
    equipment, 21-22
Safety pads, 22
Seatpost, 20
Skyway Trick Team, 26
Spoked alloy wheels, 16
Sponsorship, 55
Sprocket Rockets BMX

Freestyle Trick Team, 23, 55, *56*
Steel pedals, 20
Street riding, 65

Teams, 54-57
    competition, 60
    money earned by, 61
Television commercials, 62
Tires, 18
Track stand, 31-32, *59*
Tuff Wheels II, 18

Uniforms, 55

Wheelies, 15, 27, *29*
Wheels, bicycle, 16, 18
Wheel stand, 34, *35*

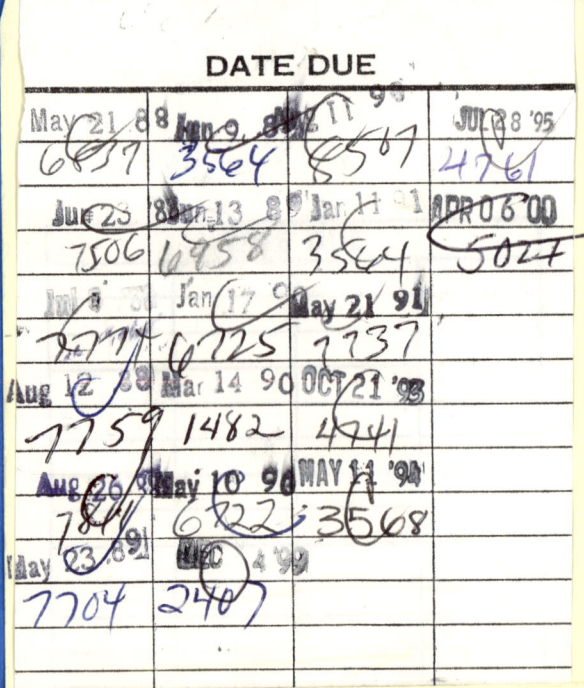